insight text guide

Brigid Magner

Don't Start Me Talking

Lyrics 1984–2004

Paul Kelly

First published in 2005, reprinted in 2008, 2020 (with minor revisions).

Insight Publications Pty Ltd
3/350 Charman Road
Cheltenham VIC 3192
Australia
Tel: +61 3 8571 4950
Fax: +61 3 8571 0257
Email: books@insightpublications.com.au

www.insightpublications.com.au

Paul Kelly's Don't Start Me Talking / Brigid Magner

Brigid Magner asserts the moral right to be identified as the author of this work.

ISBNs:
9781920693992 (print)
9781922525161 (digital)
9781922525154 (bundle: print + digital)

Cover design by Gisela Beer

Printed in Australia by Ligare

contents

CHARACTER TABLE

Characters and relationships in *Don't Start Me Talking*

Character types	Relationships & themes	Song examples
Fathers	Relationships between fathers and their children are frequently described, emphasising the importance of inheritance.	'Before the Old Man Died' 'Adelaide' 'Deeper Water' 'Going About My Father's Business'
Lovers	Platonic and carnal aspects of love are experienced by Kelly's characters; infatuation and loss are common themes.	'Look So Fine, Feel So Low' 'Don't Explain' 'Winter Coat'
	Lyrics often feature a male character who is successful in love due to sheer persistence.	'I'll Be Your Lover Now' 'Before Too Long'
Indigenous Australians	The issues of Aboriginal land rights and reconciliation are explored.	'Maralinga (Rainy Land)' 'From Little Things Big Things Grow' 'Bicentennial'
Addicts	Characters who are addicted to drugs, drinking and/or love.	The *Post* album
Criminals & outlaws	Criminals on the run: they are usually victims of injustice who are standing up for their rights.	'I Won't Be Your Dog Anymore' 'Our Sunshine' 'Pigeon/Jundamurra'
Ghosts	Ghostly presences may trigger memories of the past, or console the bereaved.	'Invisible Me' 'Cities of Texas' 'Ghost Town'
Heroes	Notable Australians whom Kelly admires and celebrates in song:	
	cricketer Don Bradman	'Bradman'
	Aboriginal activist Vincent Lingiarri	'From Little Things Big Things Grow'
	guitarist Charlie Owen	'Charlie Owen's Slide Guitar'
	weightlifter Dean Lukin	'Cool Hand Lukin'
Doubles & doppelgängers	Men who have two aspects to them, but who are largely unaware of their bad side; they may discover their true nature only through other people's stories.	'Stories of Me' 'Sweet Guy' 'I Don't Remember a Thing'

OVERVIEW

Paul Kelly is a well-known Australian musician and songwriter who has been producing music for several decades. He has written some of the most important and memorable songs in Australian popular music and has collaborated on many theatre productions and films. Although it is best known in Australia, his work has also been praised internationally. David Fricke, the US music editor of *Rolling Stone*, once described Paul Kelly as one of the finest songwriters he had ever heard, Australian or otherwise. Kelly has been described as a 'navigator of the soul', a title he has modestly denied, saying that he's 'just a song and dance man'.[1]

Kelly captures aspects of Australian life in many iconic songs like 'From St Kilda to Kings Cross' and 'Adelaide', the lyrics of which have also been read as poetry. Especially since the publications of his lyrics in two volumes, *Lyrics* (1993) and *Don't Start Me Talking* (2004), Kelly's writing has been increasingly acknowledged as having literary merit. In a review of *Lyrics*, Imre Salusinszky described Kelly as 'Australia's premier singer-songwriter for grown-ups, but also one of our two or three essential poets'.[2]

Kelly is attracted to the great stories, like those from the Bible or Shakespearean plays, yet he is also interested in the minutiae of the everyday. His keen observation of human foibles and his ear for vernacular speech is registered everywhere in his songwriting practice. A cast of believable characters emerges throughout Kelly's songs. When the lyrics are read as a collection, these character types seem more fully defined and Kelly's recurrent preoccupations become evident. Although love songs outweigh all other kinds in number, Kelly is especially interested in representing characters in moments of crisis. They struggle

---

[1] Doug Aiton, 'Dancing in shadows', *The Age*, 10 May 1998.

[2] Imre Salusinszky cited in Robert Adamson, 'Introduction', in Paul Kelly, *Lyrics*, Angus & Robertson, Sydney, 1993, p.iii.

with their identities and regret their thoughtless actions. Often there is a degree of reflection as the narrator considers the implications of past events.

Kelly is famous for his storytelling songs about love, politics and sporting heroes. Since his lyrical oeuvre has had a personal focus, mostly centred on sexual politics, he tends to attract very little adverse media attention, even when he comments on controversial current affairs. Kelly's popularity is perhaps mostly due to his ability to capture the experience of the common person trying to determine life's underlying meaning or pattern. Many Australians remember at least one Kelly song that stirs their emotions, and his songs are like anthems of Australian life, connecting people of very different ages, cultures and social groups.

BACKGROUND & CONTEXT

About Paul Kelly

The sixth of nine children, Paul Kelly was born in Adelaide in 1955. In the early 1920s, his grandparents founded the first Italian grand opera company in Australia. His grandfather, Count Ercole Filippini, was a leading baritone for the La Scala Grand Opera Company. Contessa Filippini was the first woman to conduct a symphony orchestra in Australia. Their daughter, Kelly's mother Josephine, was also a singer, but was too busy bringing up her children to concentrate on artistic pursuits.

Kelly attended a Christian Brothers school in Adelaide, where he played the trumpet and captained the cricket team. He studied arts at Flinders University in 1973, but left after a year, disillusioned with academic life. He began writing prose and started a magazine with some friends. While travelling around Australia for a few years, Kelly worked odd jobs and learned to play the guitar. He made his public debut singing the Australian folk song 'Streets of Forbes' to a Hobart audience in 1974, and two years later moved to Melbourne, where he participated in the thriving pub-rock scene. From there he went on to produce over twenty albums with an array of musicians.

Kelly has twice been awarded best male performer by the Australian Record Industry Association (ARIA) and has been honoured in the ARIA Hall of Fame. In 1999, the Australasian Performing Rights Association – the songwriters' guild – recognised Kelly's achievements by naming him songwriter of the year. His songs have also been covered on tribute albums: *Women at the Well* by well-known female singers, *Before Too Long* and *Stories of Me (a Songwriters' Tribute to Paul Kelly)*.

The ballad tradition

Although Paul Kelly's writing has emerged from a range of influences, his work needs to be read in terms of Australian literary and musical traditions, especially the ballad form. In fact, ballads are one of the earliest forms of literature. The word 'ballad' comes from an Old French word referring to a song accompanying a dance. Originating in folk songs or orally transmitted poems, ballads tell, in a direct and dramatic manner, a popular story, usually derived from a tragic incident in local history or legend. British settlers brought the ballad tradition to Australia in the eighteenth and nineteenth centuries. While the ballad died out in Britain, it became a strong component in the Australian storytelling and popular music traditions, especially in rural Australia. Subsequently, the ballad was incorporated into the Australian literary tradition.

Ballads and Australian poetry

The ballad tradition in Australia has been closely aligned with the large Irish population that immigrated in the nineteenth century. Irish ballads of this time are typically anti-establishment, usually featuring a working-class hero who is persecuted by authority figures such as landowners. They often celebrate convicts and bushrangers, who were seen by the immigrant Irish to resist the English ruling class.

The bush ballad, through its emphasis on simple emotion, realistic description and anecdote, provided early settler Australians with a way of passing on stories. The ballad emerged as the first literary form in which writers interpreted the Australian experience for their compatriots. It features in the works of Henry Lawson and AB ('Banjo') Paterson, whose *Man from Snowy River and Other Verses* (1895) includes the famous poem 'Waltzing Matilda'. A story about an ordinary man struggling to survive, 'Waltzing Matilda' has become the nation's unofficial national anthem. The themes presented in the early ballads are also explored in the short stories of Lawson and Barbara Baynton and in the songs of many Australian songwriters. In particular, country music – which has always occupied a central position within Australian popular music – has been profoundly influenced by the ballad tradition.

Paul Kelly's place within the ballad tradition

The ballad continues to be an important component within contemporary Australian music, including the work of Paul Kelly. The narrative drive in his songs connects him with early Australian balladeers, though his emphases may be different. While Kelly is concerned primarily with the lives of Australian urban dwellers, his work is not confined to any one place – a quality that makes his songs iconic to Australians, in the same way as Paterson's 'Waltzing Matilda' is. In fact, collaborator Renee Geyer has said of Kelly: 'He is the voice of urban Australia, the modern-day Banjo Paterson',[3] placing him firmly in the Australian ballad tradition.

Though they do not have the traditional ballad structure and are often sung in an Anglo-American rock style, many of Kelly's songs express concerns that are typical of the ballad tradition. He gives voice to experiences that are not written down, such as the responses of Aboriginal people to nuclear tests at Maralinga and the land rights struggle of the Gurindji. As is typical of the ballad form, Kelly often sings about current events of significance to working-class and marginalised Australians. His piece 'Emotional', about the plight of an asylum seeker in a detention centre, reveals his ongoing commitment to such causes.

Kelly's lyrics range from the political to the personal, sometimes combining the two – for instance, the political is often seen from a personal perspective. They are often suffused with loss and nostalgia, using ballad techniques to evoke a melancholy tone. Though some of Kelly's songs may be judged to be overly sentimental, this quality is typical of the urban ballad and is present in much contemporary popular music.

[3] Renee Geyer cited in Claudia Sammut, 'The gentle dreams of an urban troubadour', *Herald Sun*, 15 August 1999.

GENRE, STRUCTURE & STYLE

Genre

In the foreword to the first published edition of Paul Kelly's lyrics, acclaimed poet Robert Adamson makes the point that the earliest poets – the authors of Greek and Roman epics such as *The Odyssey* – were performance artists. The word we use for a short poem, 'lyric', originally meant a poem to be performed to the accompaniment of a lyre (a small harp). We might therefore say that Paul Kelly practises a more traditional version of the craft of poetry than most contemporary poets. Several songs may be read quickly in one sitting but, like poems, they take time to be completely deciphered.

Narrative points of view

Kelly's songs tend to be written in the first person, from one character's point of view. Sometimes they are written in the third person, as a story told by an omniscient narrator. Alternatively, they may seek to document the experiences of a number of people, assuming a play-like dialogic structure. 'She Answers the Sun (Lazybones)' and 'He Can't Decide' are examples of this technique. In this way, Kelly is able to replicate the dynamism of a conversation involving multiple characters.

Song structure

While he occasionally experiments with form, Kelly's lyrics tend to have a standard rhyming structure and chorus, or repeated refrain. The choruses differentiate these lyrics from most contemporary poetry, which is less dependent on a conventional rhyming pattern. The chorus serves to link together all the elements of a song, distilling its meaning to a few words. Kelly's lyrics are usually written with the music in mind and vice versa, further highlighting the difference between the writing of songs and the composition of poetry.

Kelly's songwriting process

In the preface to the 1999 edition of *Don't Start Me Talking,* Kelly discusses the process of songwriting in some detail. A song begins with what he calls 'dream words', which come to his mind when he starts conceiving a song, and which then undergo a metamorphosis:

> [They] fall from grace, from possibility to actuality, from dream words to real words, the real words always a little disappointing at first, bald and skinny until they are sung over and over again and the dream words disappear and the real words approach sound again.[4]

Kelly's political songs have a slightly different genesis. He calls these the 'newspaper songs' because they are often prompted by something he has read in the media. With these political songs he usually has a clearer idea of what he's writing before he starts. Kelly distinguishes his overall approach from that of a more politically orientated songwriter such as Mandawuy Yunupingu of Yothu Yindi, with whom Kelly collaborated on 'Treaty'. Kelly describes Yunupingu as: 'a big picture writer, that's how he sees his songwriting. He's a teacher; he's spreading a message, explaining a philosophy'. In contrast, Kelly sees his own songwriting as 'much fuzzier'.[5]

The song 'Nothing but a Dream', which features a muse who provides inspiration, could be read as a meditation on Kelly's own songwriting process. Other pieces, like 'Love Never Runs on Time' and 'Before the Old Man Died', feature protagonists who make up songs as a way of understanding their experiences.

---

[4] Paul Kelly cited in Claudia Sammut, 'The gentle dreams of an urban troubadour'.

[5] Paul Kelly cited in Andrew Stevenson, 'Blue Notes', *The Age*, 5 October 2001.

Unlike many contemporary singer-songwriters, Kelly avoids writing lyrics that are directly autobiographical. He claims not to be interested in revealing himself through his music – although he admits there is a subterranean story running beneath the lyrics. He does write about himself occasionally, but only in an indirect way. He has repeatedly claimed that he merely inhabits characters, like a writer of fiction:

> A lot of the songs will start from something in real life, some true detail, a real detail, not necessarily from my life. Once they start becoming songs they become fiction ... Like any writer, I'll grab anything that's at hand in order to write a song ...[6]

Literary references

The epigraph to *Don't Start Me Talking* is a quotation from the Russian writer Anton Chekhov, and it provides a clue to Kelly's writing practice: 'I don't have what you would call a philosophy or coherent world view so I shall have to limit myself to describing how my heroes love, marry, give birth, die and speak'. Through these characters and their experiences, Kelly develops a kind of commonsense philosophy which is delivered in an accessible way.

Kelly also borrows from and alludes to the work of a wide range of literary authors, including William Shakespeare, Brendan Behan, Raymond Carver, Ernest Hemingway and Edgar Allan Poe. Kelly is obviously well-read, yet he keeps the lyrics simple and intelligible, if occasionally puzzling. Indeed, Kelly likes the songs to have a certain amount of ambiguity so that the more you listen to them, the more they will reveal.

[6] Paul Kelly cited in 'From St Kilda to Kings Cross', *TNT*, 10 August 1999.

Style

Transformation and versatility

During his extensive career, Kelly's music-making has undergone a number of transformations. He began as an independent pub-rock act and now claims a range of styles as his own. Kelly calls himself a pop artist because this is a broad enough description to include styles such as rock-and-roll, dance, folk, soul, gospel and bluegrass. It may be argued that his longevity as a musician is due to this ability to adapt as musical tastes and fashions change.

The tone of Kelly's lyrics tends to vary according to which musical style he is adopting and vice versa. For instance, when he writes about sex he often draws on the Motown tradition, because musicians who recorded for the Motown Record Company wrote and sang about joy and sex without being banal. On the other hand, when he draws on the classic singer-songwriter tradition, the songs tend to be about unrequited love and relationships going wrong.

Kelly's versatility is evident in the two quite different albums that were released in 1999: a bluegrass album with Uncle Bill called *Smoke*, and a technology-influenced album as part of a new group, *Professor Ratbaggy*. *Smoke* has a distinctly hillbilly flavour, featuring a mixture of old and new songs – the old ones redone in the bluegrass style – as well as country instruments (such as the mandolin, fiddle, banjo, stand-up bass and acoustic guitar) and harmonies.

Collaboration

Collaboration is an important part of Kelly's practice as a songwriter and allows him to experiment further with style. Kelly began 'mixing things up' when he worked with Archie Roach and the Aboriginal band Yothu Yindi in 1991. An early fan of Roach's, he co-produced the singer-songwriter's acclaimed debut album, *Charcoal Lane*, with Steve Connolly. The Yothu Yindi connection was established on a trip to the Northern Territory when Kelly collaborated with the group on 'Treaty', a song that became a surprise pop hit when it was remixed as a dance single.

Kelly has said that he collaborates with other musicians to keep his own writing fresh. A number of musicians have asked him to write songs for them, including Renee Geyer, Vika and Linda Bull, Joe Camilleri and Jenny Morris. Kelly believes that this process allows him to take on different perspectives:

> As a songwriter, I'm always trying to write different types of songs anyway. I'm not a great stylist in any way ... I don't have a particular style and if I have any strength it's being able to write in different styles. It's a bit of a tightrope act: you have your own sound, you develop it, and there's a time where you have to start breaking away from it.[7]

[7] Paul Kelly cited in Shaun Carney, 'Kelly Country', *Rolling Stone* (Aus), no. 498, July 1994.

SONG-BY-SONG ANALYSIS

Post (1985)

'From St Kilda to Kings Cross' (p.3)

This is one of Kelly's best-known songs, and celebrates his adopted city of Melbourne. The narrator retreats into his mind while travelling on a bus; he prefers the run-down St Kilda beachscape to the flashiness of Sydney Harbour.

'Incident on South Dowling' (pp.4–5)

The narrator expresses a sense of shock following his girlfriend's death from a drug overdose.

'Look So Fine, Feel So Low' (p.6)

The speaker is being supported by a wealthy woman who doesn't demand much from him, but he experiences feelings of emptiness. The disjunction between appearances and reality is a frequent concern of Kelly's.

'White Train' (p.7)

This song has a hallucinogenic quality, implying that the speaker is on drugs. The term 'white train' could be interpreted as a metaphor for heroin. The narrator asks why his friend/lover has to be on the 'white train', which suggests a desire to get off it.

'Luck' (p.8)

Once again the 'train' may be seen as a drug metaphor. One possible reading is that the narrator can't give up heroin while his girlfriend already has, therefore the relationship must end.

'Blues for Skip' (p.9)

A more overt song about drug-taking. The speaker complains that there's 'no water in the well', which means that there is a drug drought. The little cloud may stand for the high the narrator is chasing, which has moved on.

'Adelaide' (p.10)

The speaker remembers the boredom of childhood in suburban Adelaide and the death of his father which left him feeling numb. He triumphantly claims 'I own this town' but his ambivalent relationship with the city is characterised by both fondness and loathing.

'Satisfy Your Woman' (p.11)

The narrator gives his fellow men advice on how to maintain relationships with women.

'(You Can Put Your) Shoes Under My Bed' (p.12)

The subject of this song is a charismatic woman who demands adoration. The lyrics are full of clichés which are cleverly undercut with humour.

'Standing on the Street of Early Sorrows' (p.13)

A lament for the speaker's summer romance as a young man. He reminisces about the heat of the summer, walking to the swimming pool and his lost girlfriend.

'Little Decisions' (p.14)

The narrator offers a brand of folk wisdom, giving simplistic solutions to life's problems.

'Cool Hand Lukin' (written with Paul Hewson, p.15)

This song pays tribute to one of Kelly's sporting heroes. Dean Lukin won the heavyweight weightlifting gold medal for Australia at the 1984 Olympics. Kelly takes the final moments of the competition and focuses on the response from the locals in Lukin's hometown of Port Lincoln.

'Laughing Boy' (for Brendan Behan, p.16)

This song is based on the poem of the Irish writer, Bendan Behan, celebrating the life of Michael Collins, the Irish freedom fighter. The laughing boy in Behan's poem, as in Kelly's song, is Michael Collins. The repeated refrain 'walking on the water' conveys the holy status of Collins, who is worshipped by some Irish people with an almost religious zeal.

Key point

Kelly is interested in the contradictions inherent in human thought, especially the dissonant messages which compete in the mind of any individual.

'Give Me One More Chance' (p.17)

A man begs for another chance from his partner, admitting his many mistakes. There is an air of inevitable failure in his pleading tone.

Gossip (1986)

'Last Train to Heaven' (p.21)

The recurrence of trains in Kelly's work indicates a preoccupation with travel as a metaphor for mental states (which can also refer to drug-taking). The invocation to the 'people' is reminiscent of gospel music.

'Leaps and Bounds' (written with Chris Langman, p.22)

This song is about an epiphany, or private revelation; it is strongly located in the physical environment through references to Melbourne landmarks such as the MCG and the Nylex clock.

'Before the Old Man Died' (p.23)

A son recalls his father as a repressive, angry figure who victimised his wife and children.

'Down on My Speedway' (p.24)

This song has a speedy energy to it, crackling with sexual tension. 'My speedway' may be read as symbolic of the narrator's desire for Suzie.

'Randwick Bells' (p.25)

The feeling of a lazy Saturday morning in bed interrupted only by church bells ringing is captured by this song – one of several about men and women enjoying each other's company and ignoring the rest of the world. Randwick is a Sydney suburb.

'Before Too Long' (pp.26–7)

The narrator is an alienated, obsessive character who is essentially stalking the woman of his dreams. 'Every dog will have his day' conveys the narrator's view of himself as an underdog, 'battler' type.

'I Won't Be Torn Apart' (p.28)

A man's statement of strength during a relationship breakdown, this is a meditation on the resilience of the human spirit amid adversity.

'Going About My Father's Business' (p.29)

This song is about inheritance and the ways in which we may repeat our parent's behaviour. The speaker goes away to war as his father had, neglecting his own son in the process.

'Somebody's Forgetting Somebody (Somebody's Letting Somebody Down)' (p.30)

The lyrics refer to the carelessness of lovers and their tendency to betray loved ones. The theme of jealousy, which bedevils many of Kelly's male protagonists, is evident here.

'The Ballroom' (p.31)

The speaker describes the difficulties of meeting his ex-girlfriend's new partners.

'Tighten Up' (p.32)

A story of impoverished working-class life. The chaotic household includes a drunken father and a fugitive son.

'I've Come for Your Daughter' (p.33)

The speaker plays on the fears of a young woman's parents. His tone is menacing; he is on their stairs and there's 'no prevention' – in other words, he will not be discouraged.

'So Blue' (for Paul Cézanne, p.34)

The speaker is transfixed by the painting of the Lac d'Annecy (Lake Annecy) in France; he admires the artist Paul Cézanne, who toiled away without much recognition during his lifetime.

'The Execution' (p.35)

The French lyrics 'Voici le temps des assassins' (meaning 'this is the time of the assassins') are from Arthur Rimbaud's poem 'Matinée d'ivresse'. These words could be the cry of a revolutionary fighter.

'Maralinga (Rainy Land)' (pp.36–7)

The person speaking first is an Aboriginal man named Yami Lester, a real person who was blinded by radioactive fallout from British nuclear testing at Maralinga in the 1950s. This is one of Kelly's songs dealing with political issues involving Aboriginal people.

'Darling It Hurts' (p.38)

The narrator is distressed to see his lover publicly prostituting herself. The theme of sexual jealousy is evident here.

'Stories of Me' (p.39)

A man living a double life compares himself to the main character in Robert Louis Stevenson's novel *The Strange Case of Dr Jekyll and Mr Hyde* (1886), because his drinking causes his character to split into a good and a bad aspect.

'Don't Harm the Messenger' (p.40)

The speaker advises us not to hurt the teller of an unpleasant truth. The messenger's journey is perhaps a metaphor for the struggle a friend may experience in conveying difficult news.

'Gossip' (p.41)

Instead of condemning gossip, the speaker depicts it as an essential part of everyday life.

'After the Show' (p.42)

Filled with an infectious sense of anticipation, this song describes the feeling of looking forward to a night out on the town.

'Bradman' (pp.43–5)

A celebration of Sir Donald Bradman's cricketing career. The speaker compares the days of 'gentleman's cricket' with the game in the present.

Under the Sun (1987)

'Dumb Things' (p.49)

The narrator catalogues his mistakes – another instance of Kelly's sympathy for the ordinary person who gambles to improve his situation. The non-narrative structure shows the disordered nature of the speaker's thoughts.

'Same Old Walk' (pp.50–1)

The narrator recognises a former lover at the airport and optimistically hopes to win her back.

'Big Heart' (p.52)

Kelly uses the metaphor of a V8 engine under the hood of a wooden car to describe a woman with a big heart.

'Don't Stand So Close to the Window' (written with Alexander McGregor, p.53)

The speaker tells the story of an illicit relationship which has to be kept indoors, since others would disapprove. The reference to the famous Ash Wednesday bushfires locates the song in Victoria.

'Forty Miles to Saturday Night' (p.54)

This song expresses the joy of anticipating a weekend after a hard week of labour. The speaker is a rural worker.

'I Don't Remember a Thing' (p.55)

The narrator experiences memory loss: accused of killing his girlfriend, he has the uncanny sense that he has been at the murder scene.

'Know Your Friends' (p.56)

Two friends rely on each other despite their differences. One is unable to confess his feelings for the other.

'To Her Door' (p.57)

A man's relationship ended due to his unemployment and alcoholism; now he hopes to be reunited with his family. The recurrent image of 'the door' represents the different phases of the relationship; the 'Silvertop' taxi locates the story in Melbourne.

'Under the Sun' (p.58)

The speaker remembers days of easy friendship which are now in the past.

'Untouchable' (p.59)

The narrator is preoccupied with a woman whose flirtatious ways continually threaten other relationships.

'Desdemona' (p.60)

In Shakespeare's play *Othello*, Othello murders his wife Desdemona because he suspects her of infidelity. This song is a moral tale about men being undone by jealousy.

'Happy Slave' (p.61)

A domineering woman takes advantage of the speaker's goodwill. 'She keeps me at my business until I'm breaking down' could refer to sexual activity which is all-consuming.

'Crosstown' (p.62)

This song depicts a relationship between lovers from different social classes – the speaker is working at two jobs to earn enough so he will eventually win the girl's hand from her affluent father.

'Bicentennial' (p.63)

Kelly juxtaposes the scene of a ship reaching the Australian shore in a re-enactment of the European landing with an image of an Aboriginal man hanging dead in a gaol cell. The narrator refers to other victims of colonialism and asks not to be included in any celebrations, as this would amount to dancing on the victims' graves.

'Ghost Town' (p.64)

A man sees the ghost of his dead child: the landscape seems desolate without her.

'Already Gone' (p.65)

Falling into a person's embrace is seen as a kind of disintegration: the speaker is smothered by desire rather than enlivened by it.

'Special Treatment' (pp.66–7)

'Special treatment' refers here to the wrongs done to Aboriginal people. The speaker is a member of the Stolen Generations who was taken away from his family.

So Much Water So Close to Home (1989)

'You Can't Take It With You' (p.71)

Kelly catalogues all the human attributes and possessions that can't be taken to the afterlife. The message is that it is better to focus on living well than accumulating assets.

'Sweet Guy' (pp.72–3)

Two lovers are in bed. Their bliss is contrasted with accounts of the man's dangerously changeable behaviour.

'Most Wanted Man in the World' (p.74)

The life of an ordinary man is transformed by his girlfriend's love, which makes him feel invincible.

'I Had Forgotten You' (p.75)

An older man apologises for having forgotten about a former girlfriend.

'Stupid Song' (p.76)

The speaker is infatuated with a woman, who is compared with a stupid song that sticks in his head.

'South of Germany' (p.77)

An older woman reflects on how her life might have turned out differently, had she taken a different path. She seems to be saying goodbye to the world before dying.

'Careless' (p.78)

The speaker apologises to his partner for being careless with her affections. He acknowledges that she 'brought [him] back' from depression.

'Moon in the Bed' (p.79)

The speaker compares his girlfriend to the sun, the moon and the stars.

'No You' (p.80)

A man experiences a profound sense of loss when his girlfriend leaves.

'Everything's Turning to White' (pp.81–2)

Inspired by the short story 'So Much Water So Close to Home' by US author Raymond Carver, the song is narrated by a woman thinking of her husband's recent fishing trip. She is chilled by his attitude to the discovery of a woman's body. The story haunts her, making her feel differently towards her husband.

Key point

Kelly's songs are often preoccupied with figures who are experiencing some kind of identity crisis, as in this song where a woman feels 'frozen inside' (p.81).

'Pigeon/Jundamurra' (p.83)

A white officer in colonial Australia hunts unsuccessfully for an Aboriginal freedom fighter named Pigeon, or Jundamurra, who declared war on white invaders in the West Kimberleys and prevented settlement for six years.

'Cities of Texas' (p.84)

Evokes the deserts and mountains of Texas and the wind that effortlessly covers expanses of time and space.

'Hard Love' (p.85)

The narrator declares his need for a 'hard love' that won't disappear.

'Beggar on the Street of Love' (p.86)

A man is humbled by his need for love: he asks in vain to be acknowledged by the woman he adores.

'Hidden Things' (p.87)

A woman describes the 'hidden things' which people trade in relationships. For her, the ability to impart secrets is more important than good looks or passion, which only fade in the long term.

'Don't Say I'm No Good' (p.88)

A goodbye 'letter' to a loved one whom the speaker is leaving.

'Just a Phase He's Going Through' (p.89)

A jaded observer sees a woman's infatuation as temporary madness, created by a man's lies.

'Too Many Movies' (p.90)

A young woman meets a fellow film buff after being criticised for watching too many movies and not being sensible enough.

'I Had Too Much Loving Last Night' (p.91)

The speaker remembers last night's passion while trying to get through a working day.

'Pouring Petrol on a Burning Man' (p.92)

A hardworking man fantasises about returning to his lover.

'Other People's Houses' (pp.93–4)

A third-person spoken piece about a young boy's visits to other people's houses while his mother cleans them.

Comedy (1990)

'Don't Start Me Talking' (p.97)

A man warns his listener not to let him start talking. It is as if he has suppressed so many life experiences that he wouldn't be able to stop talking if he gets going.

'Winter Coat' (p.98)

The 'winter coat' symbolises an affair that happened many years ago. The coat is the one stable factor the narrator can rely on in a changing world. This nostalgic song depicts the transience of relationships.

'It's All Downhill from Here' (p.99)

A man who had an abusive childhood wants to face his past once and for all, with uncertain consequences.

'Brighter' (p.100)

A wild woman is questioned by an observer who worries about the repercussions of her promiscuity.

'Your Little Sister (Is a Big Girl Now)' (p.101)

The narrator remembers his wife's little sister as a girl, realising that she has grown up when he sees her with his best friend. There are hints of an unhealthy voyeurism – as if the speaker is more interested in the little sister than his own wife.

'I Won't Be Your Dog Anymore' (pp.102–3)

This song tells the story of a fugitive on the run from the law.

'Take Your Time' (p.104)

An older woman tells a younger man to slow down and enjoy what they have together.

'Sydney from a 727' (p.105)

A celebration of Sydney as seen from the air: the 'beautiful light', 'red roofs' and the waves of Bondi Beach create a picture of the passenger's view from a plane. In the last line, the narrator imagines seeing Dallas from a different plane, emphasising that Sydney is the place he knows best.

'I Can't Believe We Were Married' (p.106)

These lyrics capture the unconventional, bohemian lifestyle of a young couple who are now divorced. The former husband seems amazed that they were once so passionate and are now so polite.

'From Little Things Big Things Grow' (written with Kev Carmody, pp.107–8)

This inspiring tale is based on historical events. On 23 August 1966 Vincent Lingiarri (also spelled 'Lingiari'), a Gurindji elder, led his people off the Wave Hill cattle station operated by the Vestey pastoral organisation, in protest against their wages and conditions. Their stand against injustice attracted national publicity for Aboriginal land rights grievances. The strike developed into a seven-year campaign by the Gurindji for the return of their traditional lands and became a cause célèbre across Australia.

In 1974 the Whitlam government handed back much of the Gurindji country. Prime Minister Gough Whitlam poured earth into Vincent Lingiarri's cupped hands in a ceremony symbolising the legal restoration of their lands. This is a typical Kelly song about underdogs achieving their goals through persistence and patience.

'Blue Stranger' (p.109)

Disconnected from their usual environments, two strangers take a chance with each other.

'Keep It to Yourself' (p.110)

The narrator advises his partner, a musician, not to disclose infidelities, for the sake of their relationship.

'Invisible Me' (p.111)

The ghost-like presence might be read as a kind of haunting by a former partner, who may or may not be dead.

'Little Boy Don't Lose Your Balls' (p.112)

A comical song with a serious message; the speaker advises a boy to preserve his courage and integrity because these qualities are precious.

'Brand New Ways' (p.113)

The narrator describes a troubled relationship.

'Treaty' (written with Mandawuy Yunupingu, p.114)

A protest song that asserts the need for a treaty between Aboriginal and non-Aboriginal Australians. The year of Australia's bicentenary, 1988, became the occasion for many protests about the dispossession of Aboriginal people.

'When I First Met Your Ma' (pp.115–16)

A father talks to his child about his courtship of the child's mother.

'Rally Round the Drum' (written with Archie Roach, pp.117–18)

Written from the perspective of an Aboriginal boxer in a circus, the lyrics convey the speaker's fatigue and sense of entrapment.

'Don't Explain' (p.119)

An experienced older woman speaks to a younger man. She ends with an open-ended offer to see him again, in a non-exclusive arrangement.

'Foggy Highway' (p.120)

The 'foggy highway' may be read as a metaphor for life. The lonely narrator believes that death is imminent.

'Nobody She Knows' (written with Gyan, p.121)

A woman leaves her relationship and travels to a place where she is anonymous.

'Play Me' (p.122)

A lover asks to be played like 'the wind upon a leaf' or a musical instrument.

'Between Two Shores' (written with Vika and Linda Bull, p.123)

The speaker feels he belongs in two places, suggesting that he had to leave one place to achieve independence but always missed one person in particular.

'Thanks I'll Think It Over' (written with Vika and Linda Bull, p.124)

A woman politely turns down a confident, affluent man.

Funerals and Circuses (1992)

'Until Death Do Them Part' (p.127)

A simple composition in the form of a wedding ceremony, celebrating the permanence of marriage.

'They Don't Have to Do My Dirty Job' (p.128)

A policeman complains about the impossible position he is put in by his 'dirty job'.

'Deadly' (p.129)

Narrated by an invincible, possibly Aboriginal figure, who has been victimised and abused.

'Do Right Man' (p.130)

Contrasting with the previous song, this one is about a man who lives by the law.

'Nobody Knows Nona' (p.131)

An inscrutable woman is the focus of this song. She is impossible to fathom, hence her attraction.

'Never Never Never' (p.132)

The narrator struggles with an eruption of a pleasantly unfamiliar, unexpected feeling.

'I Am What I Am' (p.133)

A racist man justifies his prejudice by claiming that he simply 'call[s] a spade a spade' (p.133).

'Up Down In Out' (p.134)

The focus of the narrator's interest is gravity and the way we are affected by forces beyond our control. (Note that the French lyrics in the third stanza are simply a translation of the first stanza.)

'The Tap Song' (p.135)

A woman muses on the tapping sound of wind and rain, which reminds her of her younger days.

'Jessie's Lullaby' (p.136)

This is a lullaby for a child who has been crying.

'Finale Song' (p.137)

A reflection on the transience of life. The narrator warns that happiness and sadness will eventually pass and return again.

Wanted Man (1994)

'Summer Rain' (p.141)

The speaker's lover is compared to 'summer rain' because she comes and goes without warning. Like many of Kelly's female characters, she is mysterious and ethereal.

'She's Rare' (p.142)

The narrator is entranced by a woman. He lists the physical exertions he would undertake to satisfy his desire for her.

'Just Like Animals' (p.143)

Kelly captures the ecstatic physicality of lovers. In the tradition of rhythm and blues, bodily pleasures are celebrated in an earthy way.

'Love Never Runs on Time' (p.144)

This song centres on a car trip in which the protagonist thinks about his troubled love life, turning it into a song.

'Song from the Sixteenth Floor' (p.145)

The speaker has a reckless desire to be with a woman and lists all the painful and dangerous actions he would perform to win her love.

'Maybe This Time for Sure' (p.146)

The narrator hopes to make a fresh start and avoid all the mistakes of the past.

'Ball and Chain' (p.147)

The phrase 'ball and chain' is used here as slang for husband. The speaker must leave town due to his dubious dealings, abandoning his loyal girlfriend.

'You're Still Picking the Same Sore' (p.148)

The narrator rebukes a couple for being unable to resolve their differences.

'Everybody Wants to Touch Me' (p.149)

In the conventional reading of this song, the speaker is understood to be a pregnant woman. Alternatively, it could be read as a comment on celebrity and the way it can consume a person's life.

'We've Started a Fire' (p.150)

A new relationship is compared to a fire started by children playing with matches.

'Lately' (written with Renee Geyer, p.151)

The speaker describes falling in love as a 'secret spell' which causes vagueness and a sense of wonder.

'Nukkanya' (p.152)

A song about the pain of leaving a loved one. A sense of resignation is balanced by hopefulness about the prospect of returning.

'Melbourne Girls' (p.153)

The narrator consoles a 'Melbourne girl' after a recent disappointment.

'I Was Hoping You'd Say That' (pp.154–5)

This spoken-word piece recounts the dialogue of a couple getting to know each other. A playful and experimental song which is often performed for its humour, showing Kelly's range as a performer.

'Cradle of Love' (p.156)

The narrator's 'cradle of love' is offered as a healing place where troubles may be forgotten.

'I Didn't Know Love Could Be Mine' (p.157)

The appearance of love is compared with unexpected natural phenomena like lightning and thunder. This song has many religious references: love is seen as capable of performing miracles, like healing the sick and turning water into wine.

'The Cake and the Candle' (p.158)

This song plays on the old expression about having your cake and eating it; the speaker wants the candle as well as the cake, in spite of the potential repercussions for the other person in the relationship.

'He Can't Decide' (pp.159–61)

Written in the form of a play with lines delivered by four characters; a man struggles to decide between three women who are differentiated by body size. The women form a chorus at the end, deciding to say goodbye to him if he cannot choose between them.

'These Lies' (written with Deborah Byrne, p.162)

A young girl has been abused by her grandfather. Her early loss of innocence is lamented, yet there is hope for the future based on honesty and new love.

Deeper Water (1996)

'Blush' (p.165)

An unashamedly sexual song about the narrator's compulsion to see his lover register her desire through blushing.

'Extra Mile' (p.166)

A lover asks a series of questions to gauge his partner's commitment to the relationship.

'I'll Forgive but I Won't Forget' (p.167)

The narrator laments the betrayal of a close friend and his girlfriend.

'Deeper Water' (pp.168–9)

A boy's progression to manhood is depicted using water imagery. Each stage of his life cycle is marked by a significant event which propels the protagonist into another, more mature phase.

'Madeleine's Song' (p.170)

Written for Kelly's daughter, this song tells her how much he cares for her. Such devotion is undercut by the more pragmatic last line: 'My, my Madeleine, you never let me sleep.'

'Difficult Woman' (p.171)

Composed for Renee Geyer, this song celebrates the 'difficult woman' who is 'better and worse' than other people. Knowing her is hard work but also rewarding.

'Give In to My Love' (p.172)

A tenacious suitor compares his love to extreme objects and situations.

'I've Been a Fool' (p.173)

A conflicted man finally sees through his partner's charm and decides to say goodbye.

'Anastasia Changes Her Mind' (p.174)

Anastasia is the superstitious narrator's lucky charm: her kiss on his mirror gives him success at the races, but her affections seem as fickle as his luck.

'California' (p.175)

This song is a homage to California, a dangerously beautiful place the narrator dreams about.

'Gathering Storm' (p.176)

The speaker has a dream full of omens. He wakes, worrying for his loved one – possibly a lover or a child – who is out in a 'gathering storm'.

'Close' (written with Renee Geyer, p.177)

A couple meet at a party and become intimate in the taxi when they are on the way home.

'Summer Winter Spring and Fall' (written with Renee Geyer, p.178)

A man compares his partner's changing face to the seasons. A water metaphor – 'the river is high' – indicates the unpredictability of love.

'We'll Get Over It Somehow' (p.179)

The narrator has been hurt by a confrontational, unpredictable person who is likened to a cyclone that destroys everything in its path.

'Behind the Bowler's Arm' (pp.180–1)

A cricket fan arranges to meet his friend at the Melbourne Cricket Ground for the Boxing Day Test.

'Mama Shake That Thing' (written with Vika and Linda Bull, p.182)

The speaker encourages her friend to come out dancing, reminding her that she used to inspire others before becoming depressed.

'Between Two Shores' (second version, written with Vika and Linda Bull, p.183)

A reworking of this song (p.123) emphasises the role of love in anchoring people to a place.

'How to Make Gravy' (pp.184–5)

A prisoner tells his brother about his desire to be home for celebrations on Christmas Day.

'Perfect World' (written with Michael Thomas, p.186)

A heavy drinker wishes to curb his addiction and treat his partner to breakfast in bed.

'Killer Lover' (p.187)

The speaker's lover is compared to a killer. His repeated 'deaths' and 'resurrections' are akin to the biblical rebirth of Lazarus.

Words and Music (1998)

'Little Kings' (p.191)

This song suggests that Australia has not come to terms with its dark past, in particular its treatment of Aboriginal people. A critique of greed and materialism that flourish at the expense of human values, the song emphasises the need for a sense of community.

'I'll Be Your Lover now' (p.192)

In this unsettling monologue, a persistent man uses a woman's shame and 'secrets' as leverage to bargain with her for sexual favours.

'Nothing on My Mind' (p.193)

The main character quotes Ernest Hemingway, who coined the phrase 'grace under pressure' to describe his approach to a hectic life. Like many of Kelly's songs, this one captures the cadences of everyday Australian speech.

'Words and Music' (p.194)

A man reflects on musical epiphanies from his past.

'Gutless Wonder' (p.195)

The song refers to somebody who profits from other people's talent.

'Tease Me' (p.196)

A social misfit watches a stripper and dreams of taking her away.

'I'd Rather Go Blind' (p.197)

The speaker laments the end of a relationship and fears seeing his former lover with another man.

'She Answers the Sun (Lazybones)' (p.198)

An experiment with form, this song features two voices in dialogue, as in a play.

'Beat of Your Heart' (p.199)

The reference to reading Edgar Allan Poe by firelight conjures up a cosy image of blissful communion. However, the fact that Poe is famous for his horror narratives adds an element of mystery to these lyrics.

'Glory Be to God' (p.200)

This song celebrates a lover's sexual charms, thanking God for creating her.

'Saturday Night and Sunday Morning' (p.201)

The speaker describes the difference between his lover's outward appearance and her inner warmth.

'Charlie Owen's Slide Guitar' (p.202)

This song pays homage to Charlie Owen, an Australian guitar legend. The narrator implies that the Devil is waiting for Owen's soul because he traded it for his immense musical talent.

'Melting' (written with Monique Brumby, p.203)

A narrative about childhood, centred on memories of playing at the speaker's grandmother's house. The theme of melting links, past and present, emphasises the haziness of human recollections.

'Last Night I Lay Dreaming' (p.204)

A man dreams of his dead lover, wishing that she would rise from the dead and rejoin him in bed.

'High Wild Ways' (written with Spencer P Jones and Renee Geyer, p.205)

The narrator thinks of an absent partner while walking on a beach.

'Let Me In' (p.206)

The narrator tries to persuade a woman to accept his advances. He is disturbing in his intensity, especially in his reference to using voodoo.

'Be Careful What You Pray For' (p.207)

A warning that dreams do not always turn out as planned. The narrator cautions a person who seeks revenge, saying that it can backfire and hurt the avenger.

Professor Ratbaggy (1999)

'Mannish Woman' (p.211)

A man is fascinated by a mannish woman whom he compares with historical figures like Elvis and Cleopatra.

'Can't Fake It Anymore' (p.212)

The narrator is tired of hiding real feelings behind a mask.

'Coma' (p.213)

A new lover's touch makes the speaker feel as if he has been in a coma for a long time.

'Please Myself' (p.214)

The narrator's sexual frustration is evident in his tense language.

'See the Birdie Fly out' (p.215)

These lyrics are meaningless, having more in common with a children's nursery rhyme than an adult narrative.

'Rise and Shine' (p.216)

This is a simple song calling on a loved one to 'rise and shine'.

'Oh, Death' (p.217)

The speaker laments that death is always nearby.

'Moni, Make it Good' (p.218)

Moni is seen as a man's salvation – a way to escape from the 'killing floor' he inhabits.

'Love Letter' (p.219)

A lonely letter-writer hopes to make a 'deep connection' with the girl of his dreams.

Smoke (1999)

'Our Sunshine' (written with Michael Thomas, pp.223–4)

This song pays homage to Ned Kelly. The lyrics depict the scene where the bushranger is captured by police, showing his irreverent, anti-establishment character.

'Night After Night' (p.225)

A man tries to deal with the pain of a relationship break-up. He puts on a brave face during the day but this mask always slips away at night.

'Teach Me Tonight' (p.226)

A passionate young man begs a mysterious woman to teach him about lovemaking.

'Whistling Bird' (p.227)

A series of seemingly disconnected lines creates an ill-defined sense of loss.

'Taught by Experts' (p.228)

A song about a couple with a troubled history. The last few lines suggest that the tables have been turned – the speaker is now in the powerful position after having been subordinate.

'Shy Before You, Lord' (p.229)

The speaker declares his shyness in the presence of God and tries to make amends for not acknowledging him earlier.

One Night the Moon (2001)

The following songs were written for the film *One Night the Moon,* in which the daughter of a white couple goes missing, only to be found dead by an Aboriginal tracker.

'I Don't Know Anything Any More' (p.223)

The father expresses his despair after his daughter's body has been brought home. His whole way of life has been thrown into question by this tragedy. He laments that he was blind to the kindness offered to him, leading to the prolonged hunt for his daughter.

'One Night the Moon' (written with John Romeril, p.234)

This song is sung by the girl and her parents. Written in childish language, the lyrics present the moon as an appealing symbol that draws sleepers from their beds.

'This Land Is Mine' (written with Kev Carmody, p.235)

Structured like a dialogue, this song contrasts the father's possessiveness of his farm with the tracker's conception of the land. While the farmer is worried about making the land productive, the tracker sees the whole environment as part of his being. Both speakers share a fear of dispossession.

'What Do You Know?' (written with Kev Carmody, p.236)

This song is a dialogue between the mother of the lost child and the tracker. The mother suspects that the tracker is able to locate the girl's whereabouts and considers asking him for help. The tracker knows he can find the girl, but feels thwarted by his banishment from the farm.

'Unfinished Business' (written with Kev Carmody, p.237)

In this duet, the mother and the tracker sing about their unresolved grief. The mother is haunted by her child; the tracker is angry about the hypocrisy of white society.

'Little Bones' (p.238)

As the mother and the tracker find the child's body, she describes her dread of this moment. The image of 'little bones/Washed by the rain' and 'Whitened by the sun' reinforces the tragedy of the girl's untimely death.

Nothing but a Dream (2001)

'If I Could Start Today Again' (p.241)

A ballad filled with regret, conveying a longing for another chance and for God to wipe away the twenty-four hours in which the speaker's sins were committed.

Key point

Kelly's songs often give voice to the experiences of ordinary people dealing with regrets.

'Change Your Mind' (p.242)

The speaker's passion is linked to natural rhythms and phenomena. He wishes he could interfere with nature and make a spell, causing his lover to return his feelings.

'Midnight Rain' (p.243)

The sound of midnight rain symbolises the narrator's restless pre-occupation with his former lover.

'I Close My Eyes and Think of You' (p.244)

The image of a former lover provides a hardworking man with comfort and escape. He thinks of mythical places of great beauty, all of which would pale in comparison to being with this woman again.

'Somewhere in the City' (p.245)

The narrator is tortured by the idea that his lover is somewhere in the city with a 'lowdown sorry man'.

'Just About to Break' (pp.246–7)

A man is on the verge of acting destructively. There are subtle references to the way criminality is celebrated and criminals are represented in the media.

'Love Is the Law' (pp.248–9)

The message is that riches and good deeds mean nothing if you have no love.

'The Pretty Place' (p.250)

In this happy song, memories of a 'pretty place' provide escape from the narrator's everyday reality. His dimming eyes indicate that he is old and nearing death, which will reunite him with the utopia of his dreams.

'I Wasted Time' (p.251)

In his later years the narrator reflects on how he has wasted much of his life and has so little left. 'To be or not to be?' is a reference to the famous suicide speech in Shakespeare's *Hamlet*.

'Would You Be My Friend?' (p.252)

The narrator hypothetically tests the limits of his friendship, seen here in the context of the wider community.

'Smoke Under the Bridge' (p.253)

A man walks along a lonely road in search of company and somewhere safe to sleep.

'The Gift That Keeps on Giving (The Song of Sharon)' (p.254)

The speaker has a spiritual epiphany, finding a personal connection with God.

'There's Nothing Wrong with Being Wrong Sometimes' (written with Kate Ceberano, p.255)

The speaker presents an entreaty to a lover to swallow her pride and say sorry.

'Every Fucking City' (pp.256–7)

This song laments the growing homogeneity of cities in the Western world. It also describes the experience of being in love or rejected in love, and finding that every place is similar because one's loved one isn't there.

'Roll on Summer' (pp.258–9)

The sensual pleasures of a day at the beach with a Victoria Bitter beer, suntan lotion and fish and chips – the specific tastes and smells give the lyrics a realistic quality.

'You're So Fine' (p.260)

This song is driven more by rhythm than by narrative. Its few repeated lines add up to a dynamic love song.

'Surely God Is a Lover' (p.261)

An adaptation of a poem by the Australian poet John Shaw Neilson (1872–1942). The speaker claims that God must have been a lover, because he has endowed the world with so many sensual possibilities.

'This Wasn't Supposed to Happen to Me' (written with Kate Ceberano, p.262)

The protagonist speaks with disbelief about falling uncontrollably in love – previously he had only heard about this experience in songs and read about it in books.

'Throwing Good Love After Bad' (p.263)

A friend talks on the phone to a woman who remains in a bad relationship, trying to make her see how destructive her partner has been.

'Jump to Love' (p.264)

This song is an invocation to leap into love in spite of fear.

'Wish I Was a Train' (written with Troy Cassar-Daley, p.265)

The speaker wishes to be a train in order to escape from the problems in his life.

'Forty Miles' (written with Troy Cassar-Daley, pp.266–7)

The speaker sees his life in terms of a forty-mile journey. He recalls a difficult childhood journey and his grandmother's burial. Now that his own life is near its end, he feels connected to his grandmother's final words.

'Down to My Soul' (p.268)

In this tender love song, the ageing narrator treasures the bond he has with his partner.

Ways and Means (2004)

'The Oldest Story in the Book' (p.271)

Two friends, Tom and Harry, fall for the same woman, though Harry's infatuation is revealed only in the last stanza, giving the ending a surprise twist.

'Heavy Thing' (p.272)

Infatuation is compared to a heavy load in one of Kelly's more sexually explicit songs.

'Won't You Come Around?' (p.273)

A needy man begs his girlfriend to break her rule and come to see him. Love is seen as a kind of drug to which he is increasingly addicted.

'These Are the Days' (p.274)

The narrator laments that an affair will end soon. The knowledge that their time together is finite makes the relationship all the more precious to him.

Key point

Kelly's writing recognises the transience of life and love. His songs about relationships often have elements of loss embedded in them.

'Beautiful Feeling' (pp.275–6)

This song captures the joy of a newly revealed relationship which was formerly hidden from others.

'Crying Shame' (pp.277–8)

A man tries to persuade a woman to come home with him.

'Sure Got Me' (p.279)

Two people who already have partners begin their affair under a flight of stairs at a party.

'To Be Good Takes a Long Time' (p.280)

A man claims that his efforts to be good are thwarted by the Devil. He realises that being good requires more tenacity than being bad.

'Can't Help You Now' (p.281)

The narrator addresses an old flame whose life is falling apart – he has seen this pattern before and has no sympathy left.

'Nothing but a Dream' (pp.282–3)

This song tells a dreamlike story about a 'queen' who heals a lost man. Her spell cures his unnamed sickness and prompts his creative rebirth.

'Little Bit o' Sugar' (p.284)

The neighbourly gesture of borrowing a cup of sugar becomes a metaphor for sexual activity.

'Forty-Eight Angels' (p.285)

Angels cluster around the narrator's loved one as the narrator faces death.

'Your Lovin' Is on My Mind' (p.286)

The speaker considers that his girlfriend is a 'miracle' he will never understand.

'You Broke a Beautiful Thing' (p.287)

A woman reprimands a man for ruining their relationship through his carelessness. She sees how precious the relationship was, whereas he does not.

'My Way Is to You' (p.288)

A man sees his lover as his salvation in an allegorical tale about the role of love in a man's life.

'Curly Red' (p.289)

A woman known as Curly Red is depicted as passionate but flighty.

'King of Fools' (p.290)

This song might be read as a reflection on the performer's life

'Young Lovers' (p.291)

An older man suggests that the ignorance of the young is the source of their bliss, because they don't know what lies ahead.

'Big Fine Girl' (p.292)

The narrator reflects on the carnal pleasures he has known with a girl from the country.

'Cry One More Time' (p.293)

A man mourns for the end of a troubled relationship. He vows to store his memories, making them into a diamond 'so hard and everlasting' that no other person will cause him to forget his former partner.

'Passed Over' (p.294)

In this song about a near-death experience, an angel passes over the house of an ill child but leaves him alone.

'Pussy Got Your Tongue?' (p.295)

The speaker fears that his partner has been unfaithful and confronts her with jealous imaginings.

'Emotional' (p.296)

This song presents the point of view of an asylum seeker in an Australian detention centre. Here, Kelly shows the human cost of mandatory detention.

'Where Were You When I Needed You?' (p.297)

A heartbroken man rejects the advances of a lover who has let him down.

'Brighter Day' (written with Troy Cassar-Daley, p.298)

An isolated loner longs for his lover. References to 'making toast on a piece of wire' and 'drinking from an old tin cup' imply that he is destitute and homeless.

'Beautiful Promise' (p.299)

The 'beautiful promise' is a declaration of undying love which can never be completely fulfilled.

'Meet Me in the Middle of the Air' (p.300)

This song has a hymn-like quality with its references to a shepherd, green pastures, a rod and staff and being anointed with oil. It is another creative imagining of a man's death.

CHARACTERS & RELATIONSHIPS

Relationships between men and women

Key quotes

'But when I lie next to my girl/I'm the most wanted man in the world' (p.74, 'Most Wanted Man in the World')

'Never has a man been born/Who can take a woman's scorn/Nor tasted a more bitter wine/Than the brewing of his mind' (p.60, 'Desdemona')

'You put the weapon in my hand/You made me what I am' (p.228, 'Taught by Experts')

''Cause you know and I know that love never runs on time' (p.144, 'Love Never Runs on Time')

Paul Kelly has always aspired to write modern love songs but they always seem to become complicated, with other people creeping into the traditional 'boy meets girl' narrative. Vexed relationships between men and women figure in many of the lyrics. Kelly's songs about love are invariably bittersweet, revealing the joy of love as well as its pain. The protagonists are usually men, although there are a few songs written from a female perspective such as 'Taught by Experts' (p.228) and 'Don't Explain' (p.119).

Kelly is more interested in depicting the ways in which people behave than in providing a moral message. In fact, many of his characters find themselves in morally complex situations for which there is no easy solution. Recognising that people are fallible and prone to give in to temptation, Kelly's lyrics frequently address the issue of infidelity – or the threat of it. In 'Satisfy Your Woman' (p.11), infidelity is even condoned by the narrator, who claims that a man may 'stray' as long as his girlfriend knows that she's the one who matters most.

A number of songs deal with the consequences of betrayal. In 'The Oldest Story in the Book' (p.271) and 'I'll Forgive but I Won't Forget' (p.167), men are betrayed by trysts between their girlfriends and best friends. 'Keep It to Yourself' (p.110) is narrated by a woman who mocks her partner for thinking his infidelities matter in the overall scheme of things, yet there is a hurt quality to her narrative which lends the song a realistic complexity.

Sexual jealousy and power

The nature of sexual jealousy is another subject favoured by Kelly. In 'I'd Rather Go Blind' (p.197) a man claims that he would prefer to become blind than to see his ex-girlfriend with another man. His life has already been impoverished by her departure and he imagines the worse humiliation of witnessing her happiness with someone else. His mind is obviously in a disordered state, struggling to deal with his recent loss. A similar scenario is alluded to in 'Desdemona' (p.60), inspired by the Shakespearean play *Othello*. In the play, Othello is told lies by his seemingly trustworthy subordinate, Iago, which eventually drive him to strangle his loyal wife. The song, like the play, shows how jealousy can completely ruin a good man.

'Taught by Experts' (p.228) is one of a number of songs in Kelly's oeuvre that deal with a changing power dynamic within a relationship. The speaker describes herself as a 'little worm' that has turned, giving back the grief she has received in the past. Another significant example is 'Don't Say I'm No Good' (p.88), in which a man leaves home because he can no longer bear to be treated badly by a more powerful partner. Usually there's some kind of imbalance between the partners, providing an element of dramatic tension. The most frequent scenario features a man who desires a woman who isn't as interested, as seen in 'Untouchable' (p.59) or '(You Can Put Your) Shoes Under My Bed' (p.12).

The nature of love

The lyrical tone of Kelly's love songs ranges from platonic to explicitly carnal. Like a writer of love poetry, Kelly anatomises aspects of love, especially the first flush of desire. Unafraid of writing about sex, Kelly frequently describes physical encounters between lovers; 'Just Like Animals' (p.143) and 'Big Fine Girl' (p.292) are typical examples of this kind of song.

In the later albums, songs such as 'Nothing but a Dream' (p.282) seem to display a definite shift towards thoughts of mortality, which changes the emphasis on relationships. Kelly's male characters display less ambivalence about the value of love in the face of death than his female characters do.

Key point

The views expressed in his songs are not necessarily endorsed by Kelly. Instead, he sees himself as a mouthpiece for human voices of all descriptions.

Female characters

Key quotes

'Make her feel like someone/Make her feel human' (p.11, 'Satisfy Your Woman')

'You do it right/No one else could have such grace and be so spastic' (p.12, '(You Can Put Your) Shoes Under My Bed')

'Mama gets sore with the child/Who just wants to eat and then run' (p.104, 'Take Your Time')

'Even through the darkest night/She can save me from myself' (p.79, 'Moon in the Bed')

In Kelly's songs, there are certain gendered tendencies that recur, with few variations. Men are generally looking to women to set boundaries and make rules, since their own lives are chaotic. This type of woman can be a calming, healing influence who transforms the man (as in 'Nothing but a Dream', p.282). In a number of songs there are references to women being able to 'cool' the man's brain or make his thinking 'shut down' (p.141, 'Summer Rain' and p.273, 'Won't You Come around?').

Women are frequently depicted as cool and manipulative, while men are generally lovesick and vulnerable. In 'Sure Got Me' (p.279), a man is seduced by a woman who has manipulated events to suit herself.

Similarly, 'Stupid Song' (p.76) describes a man's obsessive fixation on a woman who is described as a 'melody' that plays him with 'cool control'.

Kelly repeatedly explores the differences between internal and external qualities through his portrayals of love relationships. In 'Saturday Night and Sunday Morning' (p.201), the woman is outwardly cool yet inwardly passionate: 'Like Princess Grace in Rear Window/ She's a volcano under snow'. Other women appear to be emotionally unpredictable or simply escape from the narrator. In 'Somewhere in the City' (p.245) and 'Every Fucking City' (p.256), women lead men on wild chases through urban landscapes, making them suffer in the process.

Sometimes the man realises his mistake and fights back, as in 'Can't Help You Now' (p.281). This song features an out-of-control woman who has used up all her former lover's goodwill. A similarly flighty character appears in '(You Can Put Your) Shoes Under My Bed' (p.12), but the man's response is more sympathetic in this case.

In contrast, older women are portrayed as being considerate and sensible. The female speaker in 'Take Your Time' (p.104) tells a young man to slow down and appreciate her, comparing herself to a mother who gets annoyed with a child who eats too fast. In 'Don't Explain' (p.119), a mature woman accepts with a degree of equanimity that her young lover is leaving, having experienced similar events in the past.

Collaborations with female writers

Possibly recognising that his female characters have a tendency to be two-dimensional, Kelly has entered into a number of collaborations with female musicians. 'Mama Shake That Thing' (p.182), written with Vika and Linda Bull, features a credible monologue from one female friend to another. This is an exception to Kelly's oeuvre as a whole. His work with Renee Geyer has also added depth to a number of his representations of women. 'Close' (p.177), which was co-written by Geyer and Kelly, presents a story about a couple meeting and becoming lovers in a way that is sensitive and even-handed in its portrayal of men and women.

'These Lies' (p.162), co-written by Deborah Byrne, also convincingly captures female experience. In this instance the subject is sexual abuse by the speaker's grandfather. Evidently Kelly's various collaborations have enabled him to experiment with more believable female perspectives. For instance, 'Everybody Wants to Touch Me' (p.149), a song about pregnancy, expresses a woman's exasperation with the lack of respect accorded to her body: 'Everybody wants a slice/Everybody wants to touch me/Want a little magic in their lives'.

Many of these songs, including 'Everybody Wants to Touch Me' (p.149) and 'Everything's Turning to White' (p.81), seem to appeal to female singers. This may explain why so many women chose to contribute to Kelly's tribute album, *Women at the Well*.

Male characters

Key quotes

'And I get all your good advice/It doesn't stop me from going through these things twice' (p.49, 'Dumb Things')

'I've been wrapped up in a shell, nothing could get through to me/Acted like I didn't know I had friends and family' (p.78, 'Careless')

'But he wants to get up and he wants to stay down/And he hates himself and he hates the crowd/He wants to be alone, he wants to be surrounded' (p.16, 'Laughing Boy')

Outlaws

Most of Kelly's characters are male, yet their personal qualities vary widely. As with his female characters, there are certain types that appear repeatedly. One of his favourite characters is the outlaw who lives outside society, threatening the social order. In fact, the song Kelly first performed in public was 'The Streets of Forbes', which concerns the life and death of the famous bushranger Ben Hall. Shot dead by an Aboriginal tracker named Billy Dargin, Hall aroused a great deal of public sympathy, not unlike the more famous Ned Kelly.

Paul Kelly's album *Wanted Man* features a representation of Ned Kelly on the cover, revealing his interest in these elusive figures. 'Our Sunshine' (p.223), written with Michael Thomas, celebrates the final siege in which Ned is captured, wearing his homemade metal armour. 'Pigeon/Jundamurra' (p.83) is sung from the point of view of a colonial officer who has been ordered to locate an Aboriginal freedom fighter. However, Pigeon, or Jundamurra, is an expert tracker: he leaves no traces and cannot be caught in a trap. The officer feels mortified at his failure but grudgingly admires Pigeon's ability to elude him. The real Jundamurra taunted police for years and was believed to be immortal by his people because of his ability to evade capture for so long. Among Aboriginal people, Jundamurra is still well known due to his sustained resistance to white settlement in the West Kimberleys.

'I Won't Be Your Dog Anymore' (p.102) has a similar plot, featuring a man who turns against his masters after being mistreated. There is loneliness in his tone as he wanders around the fringes of society without any comforts. All he sees is the 'distant glow' of civilisation and all he hears is his own breathing, reinforcing his sense of solitude. Figures such as these are lonely, isolated individuals who see no alternative but to survive on their own – and on their own terms.

Doubles

Male doubles (or doppelgängers) occur in several of Kelly's songs, indicating a fascination with the duality of human nature. 'Stories of Me' (p.39) is narrated by a man who is leading a double life. Since his girlfriend left he has become a drunkard who makes a spectacle of himself in public. Alcoholic rituals are the only way he knows to deal with his sadness. With no memories of his own, he discovers from other people's stories that he behaves badly after drinking. 'Sweet Guy' (p.72) is also about a changeable character who treats his girlfriend tenderly and harshly by turns. Everyone tells his girlfriend that she's crazy to stay with a man who is so cruel. She is confused by his bad behaviour and hypnotised by his attentions, finding it impossible to leave. In both these songs, the wider community has a better understanding of the man's character than he himself does

A variation on this pattern concerns a man who murders his partner but has no recollection of doing so, in 'I Don't Remember a Thing' (p.55). He sees himself in a photo with the dead woman and observes a note on the dresser that seems to indicate his guilt. The repeated refrain 'I don't remember a thing' reinforces his dreamlike state. 'Laughing Boy' (p.16) features a man, based on the Irish freedom fighter Michael Collins, who is riven by contradictions. Paralysed by indecision, he finds it impossible to know how to act in order to achieve happiness.

Identity crises

Key quote

> 'My philosophy's eclectic/Things round here are gonna get hectic' (p.247, 'Just About to Break')

Frequently, Kelly's characters are undergoing some kind of emotional trauma or identity crisis. They are often obsessive types, driven to commit a crime due to their extreme fixations. The persistent lovers in these lyrics have the capacity to become predatory stalkers if their intensity is not kept in check. 'Let Me in' (p.206) features a character who threatens to 'tear … down' a woman's 'fortress' in order to gain access to her, rather than waiting for her consent. 'Just About to Break' is written from the point of view of a man who describes himself as a 'sleeping time bomb' (p.246). His delusional state of mind is expressed through his disordered language. Immediately before the final refrain there is an unexpected line: 'My heart, my heart is full of love' (p.247), as if he has been driven to this extreme state of mind by disappointment or betrayal.

'Deadly' (p.129) has a similar tone, except the protagonist appears to be an Aboriginal man who is angry with the world because of the wrongs done to his people. In retaliation, he has become a legendary figure like Batman, Tarzan, Attila the Hun or Alexander the Great. Comparing himself with Rasputin, the Russian prophet who seemingly could not be killed, he claims to be superhuman in his invincibility.

Father figures

Key quotes

'Dad's hands used to shake but I never knew he was dying' (p.10, 'Adelaide')

'Before the old man died/Before we came alive' (p.23, 'Before the Old Man Died')

'Going about my father's business/Doing my father's time/What's done to me I'll do to mine' (p.29, 'Going About My Father's Business')

Fathers appear in many Kelly songs, in different guises, while mothers are largely absent. 'Adelaide' (p.10) is based on Kelly's memories of his father's death when he was thirteen, while 'Madeleine's Song' (p.170) is addressed to his little daughter who won't let him sleep. Other lyrics, like 'Before the Old Man Died' (p.23), have more fictional underpinnings. In this song, a man recalls his murderous hatred of his cruel father, remembering his adolescent plot to murder him. The positive outcome of this dire domestic situation is that the narrator has turned his attentions to songwriting as a form of escape, transforming anger into art.

The narrator in 'When I First Met Your Ma' (p.115) tells his son about meeting the woman who became the boy's mother, and their eventual parting. 'One Night the Moon' (p.234) and 'Jessie's Lullaby' (p.136) are written to soothe children to sleep. 'One Night the Moon' has an additional function – in the film of the same name – as a device for explaining why a little girl goes missing from her bedroom in the middle of the night. Other songs reveal a dark side to familial relations, as in 'These Lies' (p.162) about (grand)parental abuse.

'Deeper Water' (pp.168–9) concerns a man thinking about his father and reflecting on his own parenting skills. The sea is the common element joining his memories. In both narratives a father is holding his child in the sea, protecting it from harm. The sea symbolises the passing of time and the cyclical nature of human relationships. This idea is also present in 'Going About My Father's Business' (p.29), which is a universal story of duty taking precedence over familial duties. The narrator goes away to war, realising with sadness that he is repeating his own father's neglect.

The concerns of these father figures are less selfish than those of the lovers in other Kelly songs. Concerned with their performance as parents, they are more socially engaged than other character types. The appearance of children marks an entry into another phase of their lives and a growing awareness of their responsibilities.

Key point

In Kelly's songs, the presence of father figures provides an opportunity for the exploration of inheritance within families.

Friends

Key quotes

'She has a problem with some man who stayed and then ran/He's understanding but oh how his heart is breaking' (p.56, 'Know Your Friends')

'We thought we were endless, couldn't see our friendship undone/ Colourful and strange, a kind of life endangered/On the turn under the sun' (p.58, 'Under the Sun')

'Thought I loved her, hung my heart on the moon/Started howling, made no sense/Thought my friends would rush to my defence' (p.49, 'Dumb Things')

'Sometimes the very best of friends just have to disagree/I've seen the very best of friends part forever bitter company' (p.167, 'I'll Forgive but I Won't Forget')

Given that love songs form the bulk of Kelly's songwriting output, friends play a fairly minor role. Often they are seen as sources of comfort when love relationships go awry. 'Dumb Things' (p.49), one of Kelly's most memorable songs, is narrated by a gambler and risk-taker who has ignored good advice from his friends, yet expects them to save him when he falls. The implication is that he has already moved beyond them to such an extent that they are unable to help; all they can do is witness his downfall.

A number of songs feature men in pubs together as drinking buddies, but few deal specifically with closer male friendships. In 'Nothing on My Mind' (p.193), the male narrator complains about his week to a series of different men while playing pool and drinking beer. Their identities don't seem to matter to the speaker because he simply requires impersonal male companionship. Like the narrator of 'Don't Start Me Talking' (p.97), he'll talk to anyone as long as he can 'keep ripping the scab off those cold little vicious ones as they keep coming right across the bar' (p.193). Friendly conversations like this also provide an opportunity for the observation of Australian male speech, which Kelly replicates so well.

Male friends are often consulted for advice in times of trouble. Men offer their own brand of folk wisdom based on experience in 'Satisfy Your Woman' (p.11) and 'Little Decisions' (p.14). The narrator in 'Little Decisions' shows a distinct lack of tolerance, giving the impression that he is tired of hearing his friend complaining about his problems without doing anything about them. The speaker adopts a similar tone in 'Throwing Good Love After Bad' (p.263) when talking to a friend on the phone. The friend explains that all her other mates have deserted her 'one by one', which the narrator can see is because they couldn't bear to see her remain in a damaging relationship. Implying that their relationship is almost over, the narrator tells her friend that she is blind to what the rest of the world can see only too clearly.

In other songs, there is a tendency to romanticise friendships from the past and mourn their inevitable dissolution. The friends in 'Under the Sun' (p.58) have the buoyant confidence of youth, thinking their friendship is 'endless'. Set on a road trip from Fremantle, the friends discuss dreams and make up schemes that seem idealistic in retrospect. The friends are described as 'microscopic, swarming in the honey sun', as if their relationship was already undergoing an unfortunate transformation that they couldn't recognise at the time.

Male friends invariably come into conflict over women in Kelly's songs. The devoted friends in 'The Oldest Story in the Book' (p.271) eventually become estranged because they both love the same person. The friend whose love is (at least initially) unrewarded sings about the girl instead, channelling his disappointment into creativity. The story told in 'I'll Forgive but I Won't Forget' (p.167) is a more explicit dissection of betrayal by a friend. This concerns a long-term friendship that has had many 'ups and downs' but has finally come to an end. The narrator complains that he has always been the better friend, so he's not surprised that his friend has committed another betrayal. The fact that he has defended the friend against other people's criticisms seems to rankle most, since they were right all along about his friend's unreliable character. In order to defend his own honour, the narrator makes a decision to forgive but not forget what his friend has done.

'Would You Be My Friend?' (p.252) also places a friendship in its broader social context. The narrator tests his friend's loyalty by listing a range of misdemeanours and asking if he would be forgiven should he commit them. He wants to know if their private connection could survive public embarrassment and mental breakdown. This song reveals the human need for loyal companionship through good times and bad.

In 'Know Your Friends' (p.56), Kelly tackles the difficult subject of friendship between men and women, raising the question of whether or not they can be companions without an element of sexual tension. The female friend is recovering from a break-up with another man so the male friend must suppress his own romantic feelings. They are shown to have opposite natures, which means that he must always compromise, 'just to please her' (p.56). This suggests that the power balance between them is uneven, due to his infatuation.

'Difficult Woman' (p.171), written for Renee Geyer, explores the character of a 'high maintenance' friend who experiences incredible highs and lows. Her nature is described as self-protective, which is why she finds it hard to trust people. The narrator observes that a difficult woman '[s]ometimes hurts her friends when she don't mean to', so she needs 'a special kind of friend' – somebody who is forgiving of her flaws.

Key point

Incidents involving friendships on the verge of falling apart are of strong interest to Kelly. At these moments, feelings are intense and unpalatable truths, which would normally be suppressed, are voiced.

Ghostly presences

Key quotes

'And behind my eyes, my daily disguise/Everything's turning to white' (p.81, 'Everything's Turning to White')

'You might feel something rushing/It's only nothing/Just invisible me' (p.111, 'Invisible Me')

'Standing right beside me at my bed I felt your breathing/You said "Daddy can I come inside? It's cold down in the ground"' (p.64, 'Ghost Town')

Ghostly presences appear frequently in these lyrics, in the form of memories or as spirits that reveal themselves for certain reasons. Like Shakespeare, Kelly finds ghosts or apparitions useful as dramatic devices. His characters are haunted by ghosts that make their mental disorder visible, or remind them of things they may have forgotten.

In 'Everything's Turning to White' (pp.81–2), the wife of a fisherman who finds the body of a murdered woman becomes fixated on the woman's untimely death. The song shows how an incident like this can draw attention to unpleasant aspects of a person's character. The narrator cannot bear the fact that her husband and his mates discovered a body but did not report it until after the end of their fishing trip. To her, this seems to be the ultimate indignity, revealing their attitudes towards women. Gradually, the spirit of the murdered woman takes over the wife's life, changing her relationship with her husband and making her feel 'frozen inside' (p.81). Possibly the marriage had had problems before the husband's fishing expedition, but this event reveals aspects of his character that his wife can no longer ignore. While the dead woman does not appear physically, her presence is palpable throughout the narrative.

Like the wife in 'Everything's Turning to White' (p.81), the narrator in 'Ghost Town' (p.64) is haunted by a dead person. His child appears to him while he sleeps and begs to be allowed into bed because 'It's cold down in the ground'. We are left with the impression that her death has turned his whole world into a ghost town. He feels that every place he goes is the same, indicating that part of him has died along with his child.

The ghostly figure in 'Invisible Me' (p.111) flies through the air, aiming for a person as she is sleeping. It might be understood as the spirit of a former lover who has died, returning to check on their loved one. Alternatively, this spirit could be seen as a projection from the mind of a living person still obsessed with an ex-partner. A more impersonal ghostly presence is the wind in 'Cities of Texas' (p.84), a timeless wind that 'no one knows' and has been blowing long before people inhabited the earth. Speaking on behalf of the natural world, the wind warns us that our achievements are transient. The song can also be read as a comment on the practice of building cities in inhospitable places, a subject that has particular relevance to the Australian landscape.

Key point

Ghostly presences can be seen as embodiments of the psychic connections between people which may linger long after physical ties have been severed.

THEMES, IDEAS & VALUES

Mortality

Key quotes

'Dad's hands used to shake but I never knew he was dying/I was thirteen, I never dreamed he could fall/And all the great aunts were red in the eyes from crying/I rang the bells, I never felt nothing at all' (p.10, 'Adelaide')

'Soon it's closing time/Won't you stay with me?' (p.251, 'I Wasted Time')

'If I could only count my days/But I just don't know what's in store' (p.244, 'I Close My Eyes and Think of You')

'In my mind I see the light/I've never been so ready/Now I'm going to the pretty place' (p.250, 'The Pretty Place')

The characters in these songs have a variety of responses to the threat of impending death. Faced with death, a number of Kelly's characters become fearful, while others accept it peacefully. The lyrics suggest that premature death is the most difficult to accept, due to its unexpected nature. The semi-autobiographical piece 'Adelaide' (p.10) is about a boy who feels nothing at his father's funeral, unable to register the enormity of the event. Only with hindsight can the adult look back at the child and see the loss of his father more clearly.

'Oh Death', based on a traditional song, contains the repeated line, 'Oh death, oh death, won't you hold me over for another year?' (p.217). The implication is that death is always lurking, ready to prey upon the unwary. The narrator's mother tells him never to take death's remoteness for granted, hence his plea to be spared once more. 'Passed Over' (p.294), which also has a folksy, ballad-like quality, is narrated by a man who is thankful that his ill child has been left alone, after a very close call with death.

'Deeper Water' is an exploration of familial inheritance that features the untimely death of the narrator's partner: 'Death doesn't care just who it destroys/Now the woman gets sick, thins down to the bone/She says

"Where I'm going next, I'm going alone"' (pp.168–9). Death is depicted here as an indiscriminate force that can take people away at any time.

The prevalence of Kelly's songs about death has increased as he has grown older. One of the pieces revealing Kelly's later preoccupation with mortality is 'The Pretty Place' (p.250), which centres on a man's fond memories of a favourite spot. Knowing he will never see this place again, because it now exists only in his memory, he dreams of going there when he dies. In this way, his memory becomes his own private heaven and source of consolation with death imminent. The speaker in 'I Wasted Time' (p.251) realises that he has frittered his life away without having achieved anything substantial. Recognising that he does not deserve pity, he seeks some company to help him make the transition to the next world.

'I Close My Eyes and Think of You' (p.244) shows a man thinking fondly of a lover as a way of distracting himself from his uncertainty about the future. A destitute man sleeping rough in 'Brighter Day' (p.298) wishes to find a tune that will 'carry [him] away' to gaze upon a loved one's face. Music and the thought of a distant love provide him with a moment of comfort in his isolation. Given the bleakness of his situation, he invokes death, asking to be carried away to a better place where all his worries will be over. 'Meet Me in the Middle of the Air' (p.300) is narrated by a holy being who invites the listener to a house where all cares disappear. Like love, religious belief is shown to offer solace to people who are suffering from trepidation about the approach of death.

Key point

Love is often depicted as the only real consolation in the face of death.

Protesting against injustice

Key quotes

'That was the story of Vincent Lingiarri/But this is the story of something much more/How power and privilege cannot move a people/Who know where they stand and stand in the law' (p.108, 'From Little Things Big Things Grow')

'They sang my praises far and wide/But it didn't mean a thing/They saddled me with prizes/Just a swag full of nothing' (p.237, 'Unfinished Business')

'In the land of the little kings/There's a price on everything/And everywhere the little kings/Are getting away with murder ... They're so busy building palaces/They don't see the poison in the wells' (p.191, 'Little Kings')

'My home in ashes I can handle/But not to see my loved ones losing their way' (p.296, 'Emotional')

Kelly's lyrics reflect his concern with injustice, especially in the Australian context. Kelly follows in the footsteps of early balladeers with songs that tell stories about significant incidents in Australian history. The well-known song 'From Little Things Big Things Grow', co-written with Indigenous performer Kev Carmody, tells of the struggle of the Gurindji people for land rights from 1966 to 1974. This story fascinates Kelly because it involves a group of underprivileged people taking a stand against the wealthy corporation that was exploiting them. In the end, the Gurindji were victorious, due to their persistence over a number of years.

'Bicentennial' (p.63) is a stark portrayal of the disjuncture between black and white understandings of Australian history. The narrator asks not to be included in Bicentennial celebrations because they are based on a monumental lie. He alludes to the high rate of Aboriginal deaths in custody by describing the lonely death by hanging of a man called Charlie in a police cell. By contrasting this swinging body that 'won't dance any more' with the Bicentennial festivities, Kelly paints a bleak portrait of racial segregation. His interest in Australia's fugitives and 'hunted men' also emerges in this early song – a theme that recurs throughout his oeuvre.

'Special Treatment' (p.66) is another song that tackles white hypocrisy in dealings with Aboriginal people. Historical facts are told from the point of view of a contemporary Aboriginal person who lists the wrongs done to family members. The separation of Aboriginal peoples from their land and their families, and their inferior status within white society, are all mentioned. The ironic phrase 'special treatment' refers to the white notion that Aboriginal people have been treated differently 'for their own good', while the lyrics undercut this idea throughout. This song gives a human face to racial policies, allowing the listener to imagine the tragedies caused by such brutal practices.

'Little Kings' (p.191) may be read as a comment on the way Australia was being governed at the time. Some journalists have suggested that it is about the process of reconciliation, for which Kelly has offered his support. The reference to 'poisoned wells' implies that the country cannot prosper without addressing past wrongs.

One Night the Moon

In the film *One Night the Moon*, Albert, the Aboriginal tracker, sings of his anger about being undervalued by white society. Caught in a difficult position as a member of the local Aboriginal community but also obliged to work for white people, Albert feels that he gains nothing in return, except grief. He sings the duet 'Unfinished Business' (p.237) with the mother of a lost child, expressing his frustration with being both used and ostracised by white people. The fact that he eventually locates the white child's body, despite the farmer's prejudice, shows that Albert believes in doing the 'right' thing, even against the odds. The phrase 'unfinished business' refers to the characters' unhappiness but may also allude to the state of race relations in Australia more generally.

'This Land Is Mine' (p.235), from the same film, makes black/white conflict more explicit, with both the farmer and the tracker singing: 'This land is mine ... They won't take it away'. The lyrics explore the men's different conceptions of the natural environment, with the tracker claiming that the land forms an important part of his identity while the farmer is concerned about making a profit and keeping the bank at bay.

Asylum seekers

In 'Emotional' (p.296), Kelly confronts the controversial issue of asylum seekers. This song reveals the plight of asylum seekers imprisoned in Australia's detention centres. The narrator speaks of his confusion about whether or not he will ever be allowed out of this prison and be able to live in freedom. His lines, 'My home in ashes I can handle/But not to see my loved ones losing their way' show that the damage done by imprisonment to people's mental wellbeing is more serious than that done by separation from their homelands. By depicting the emotional reality of a person in this situation, Kelly draws attention to, and questions, the policy of mandatory detention.

Key point

Many of Kelly's songs feature ordinary people battling against larger forces that constrain them.

The power of memory

Key quotes

'I turn to hold her but I'm not there/Tonight I feel like both of us are made of air' (p.75, 'I Had Forgotten You')

'And the years have changed even the sound of your name/I can't believe we were married' (p.106, 'I Can't Believe We Were Married')

'Many lives I could have lived, many trails taken ... You walk into a room sometime and then a window opens' (p.77, 'South of Germany')

Memories are depicted as being capable of transporting people to a more pleasant setting, allowing them to transcend their current circumstances momentarily. 'I Had Forgotten You' (p.75) is about the failure of a man's memory and the shame this causes him. He is reminded of an old flame by a mutual friend and is besieged by thoughts of her, lending his present an air of unreality. He suddenly feels as if he and his wife are 'made of air'. The memory of his youthful girlfriend makes him feel his age and notice his wife's grey hair.

Objects can be repositories of memory that can trigger powerful feelings of nostalgia. A coat houses precious memories of a past relationship for the narrator in 'Winter Coat' (p.98). The coat becomes a poor substitute for a lost lover, but his memories, linked to the coat, keep him warm in his frosty isolation. The narrator of 'I Can't Believe We Were Married' (p.106) finds it difficult to believe that he was ever married to his ex-wife. His memories invoke a sense of wonder about the way this relationship has changed over time. They used to be passionate newlyweds leading an unconventional lifestyle; now they are mere acquaintances.

'Other People's Houses' (p.93) depicts a man's memories of visiting houses with his mother as a child. The concrete details of his recollections give the song a realistic quality, prompting listeners to imagine the scenes he describes. An older woman in 'South of Germany' (p.77) dwells on a life-changing choice made many years ago in Germany. Nearing death, she wonders what might have been if she had chosen differently. As in 'I Had Forgotten You' (p.75), the narrator feels that the person next to her in bed is barely there, while thoughts of lovers from the past are infinitely more vivid. This may be seen as a consequence of age and the way it illuminates early memories over more recent ones.

Key point

Memories cause Kelly's characters to reflect on their past and wonder about the different courses their lives might have taken.

Religion and morality

Key quotes

'She don't believe in God/or Jesus Christ our Lord/But she sure loves to call their names' (p.274, 'These Are the Days')

'To be good takes a long time/But to be bad no time at all' (p.280, 'To Be Good Takes a Long Time')

'There are things a man can't manage/And that's the devil's share' (p.14, 'Little Decisions')

'Holy night! Blessed daylight!/You are my true delight' (p.254, 'The Gift That Keeps on Giving')

References to the Bible in a number of songs indicate Kelly's sustained interest in Christian narratives. Given Kelly's interest in biblical stories it is appropriate that the title of his tribute album, *The Women at the Well*, comes from a passage in the New Testament Book of John, in which a woman is inspired by her meeting with Jesus at a well. For Kelly, the well symbolises a group of women 'drawing on one source, in this case, one songwriter'.[8]

It might be argued that Kelly's upbringing as a Catholic has played a part in forming his world view. Certainly, love is on the side of good in Kelly's oeuvre. In 'Love Is the Law' (p.248), the narrator claims to 'speak in tongues of angels', but knows that he is nothing without love. However, Kelly's spirituality is never prudish or moralistic. He often uses religious words in sacrilegious ways, as in 'These Are the Days' (p.274) and 'Surely God Is a Lover' (p.261), in which sex and God are intimately associated. Another such song, 'Glory Be to God' (p.200), celebrates sexuality while thanking God for creating it. Sometimes the lyrics use 'God' or 'Jesus' as verbal exclamations, just as people do in everyday life.

Kelly's interest in gospel music explains the presence of a few spiritual songs which are orientated around worship, such as 'The Gift That Keeps on Giving' (p.254) and 'Shy Before You, Lord' (p.229). In a slight twist to

---

[8] Paul Kelly cited in Carolyn Webb, 'Women mess with "thrilled" Kelly', *The Age*, 13 May 2002.

the conventional narrative point of view, 'Meet Me in the Middle of the Air' (p.300) is written as a speech by God to someone who is about to die, encouraging them to join him in heaven.

Asking for help

While they are not particularly religious overall, Kelly's characters tend to call out for help from God when they are in trouble. In this way, Kelly questions the selfish motives implicit in some people's notion of God. Interestingly, the lyrics do not clearly state that such a God will actually help these characters. The narrator in 'If I Could Start Today Again' (p.241) begs God to wipe away the last twenty-four hours after committing acts he now regrets. But he realises that even 'the kings and queens in the bible' couldn't turn back time, so his prayer is in vain.

Kelly's protagonists tend to realise that they are not fully in control of their lives and that some things must be left to a higher power to decide. 'Gathering Storm' (p.176) features a person, possibly a parent, worrying about somebody who may be in trouble. The phrase 'God speed' is used to bless this lost soul who is out of reach. In this way, the narrator invokes God to compensate for their own powerlessness. The delusional man in 'Just About to Break' (p.246) claims to be able to multiply 'fish and bread', like Jesus feeding the masses. Yet we know this is merely a hollow boast, based on mental instability rather than holiness.

The role of the Devil

The Devil also has a substantial role to play in Kelly's lyrics. In 'Little Decisions' (p.14), the narrator claims that things falling beyond a man's control are the 'devil's share' (p.14). In 'To Be Good Takes a Long Time' (p.280), the speaker expresses a difficulty with being good, commenting that the Devil is always close behind, prompting bad behaviour. Musical talent is often depicted as being a gift from God or as something that is won from doing a deal with the Devil. Charlie Owen, a well-known Australian guitarist, is shown to be in league with the Devil because there is no earthly explanation for his incredible ability ('Charlie Owen's Slide Guitar', p.202).

Loss

Key quotes

'Love like a bird flies away/You'll find out the only way' (p.115, 'When I First Met Your Ma')

'Once I had a place I could call my own/Now wherever I lay my head is home' (p.253, 'Smoke Under the Bridge')

'Once I knew how the world worked ... Now I don't know anything any more' (p.233, 'I Don't Know Anything Any More')

Loss figures repeatedly in Kelly's songwriting. Kelly suggests that, although loss is frequently inexplicable, it is also an intrinsic part of life – one that becomes familiar through experience. In 'When I First Met Your Ma' (p.115), love is compared to a bird that flies away, never to be seen again. A father tries to convey the nature of loss to his child, but observes regretfully that this can be learnt only through bitter experience. The defeated farmer in 'I Don't Know Anything Any More' (p.233) gives up all pretence of mastery and admits that the death of his daughter has thrown all of his certainties into question.

Loss of innocence

Some characters struggle with an early loss of innocence during a painful childhood. This is implied in 'It's All Downhill from Here' (p.99) and more explicitly stated in 'These Lies' (p.162). For these figures, loss has come prematurely, hardening them against the world. The narrator in 'It's All Downhill from Here' refers to a rough beginning in a 'crowded taxi' and an increasingly disordered childhood dominated by strangers who 'bought and sold' him. 'These Lies' considers the irrevocable damage done to a young girl by her grandfather's sexual abuse: 'Summer's sweet and budding fruit' suggests the young girl's blossoming, which is brutally cut short by 'winter's icy fingers' – that is, by her grandfather's unwanted attentions.

Relationship changes

Like several other Kelly songs, 'Before Too Long' (pp.26–7) emphasises the changeability of romantic relationships. This is seen positively by the narrator, who regards himself as an underdog who deserves a chance to experience love, even if it is at the expense of somebody else. He claims that the transience of life enables 'invisible' men to achieve their desires: 'Before too long/He who is nothing/Will suddenly come into view' (p.26).

Many of Kelly's male protagonists struggle to deal with the agony of relationship break-ups and the losses engendered by these. 'No You' (p.80) records the sensation of disbelief when the loved one is no longer present. The protagonist's mind keeps registering the harsh truth of his beloved's absence, over and over.

Loss of identity

Loss of identity is another theme that emerges in the songs about split personality ('Stories of Me', p.39; 'Sweet Guy', p.72; 'I Don't Remember a Thing', p.55). In these lyrics, men lose their sense of spiritual coherence, becoming fractured beings capable of destructive acts.

The loss of worldly possessions is sometimes depicted as a way of achieving contentment. The narrator of 'Smoke Under the Bridge' (p.253) searches for a friendly fire to warm himself by, having lost everything he once owned. There is a certain freedom in his dispossession as he can now fully appreciate the importance of human companionship. His long walk searching for company and understanding might be read as a metaphor for the lifelong journey that we all undertake.

Key point

As an observer of human behaviour, Kelly is adept at giving voice to the lost and the dispossessed.

Celebrity

Key quotes

'They're gonna want to analyse me/Canonise and demonise me/Buy the rights and serialise me/Moralise and sermonise against me' (p.246, 'Just About to Break')

'Here he comes now, gutless wonder, with his merry crew/Stepping lightly, smiling brightly, those big eyes on you' (p.195, 'Gutless Wonder')

While Kelly denies any autobiographical content to his writing, a few songs may be read as commentary on his own experience as a musician. Some songs feature characters who make music as an antidote to unhappiness or as a way of validating painful experience. The protagonist in 'Love Never Runs on Time' (p.144) turns his troubled relationship into a song, while the son in 'Before the Old Man Died' (p.23) channels his anger into art. 'The Oldest Story in the Book' (p.271) also features a musician who uses his disappointment in love as the inspiration for a love song, transforming a youthful passion into a timeless work of art. He also has the satisfaction of knowing that his song has won the heart of his lover, even if they cannot be together.

As a well-known Australian musician, Kelly is able to provide insight into celebrity life. 'You Can't Take It With You' (p.71) puts the phenomenon of stardom into perspective in the lines: 'You might have a prime-time TV show seen in every home and bar/But you can't take it with you'. The trappings of worldly success are transient and cannot be relied upon in the long run.

Kelly's body of work also contains more general observations about trends in popular culture. 'Just About to Break' (p.246) is about the public fascination with criminals. The narrator, who describes himself as a 'sleeping time bomb', claims that he's going to be analysed and demonised once he finally 'breaks'. The prevailing passion for the consumption of criminal narratives is critiqued in this song. Rather than doing anything to help a man in trouble, people would prefer to watch a movie about him. Famous criminals who have become celebrities, or vice versa, may have prompted Kelly's song on the subject. Here the celebrity is shown to be a focus for people's dissatisfactions, providing them with distractions from the tedium of everyday life. However adored he may be, the celebrity pays a high price for this rarefied lifestyle, losing something of themselves in the process.

The most overtly scathing portrayal of celebrity life is the song 'Gutless Wonder' (p.195), which could be interpreted as a critique of the media and the way it operates. The 'gutless wonder', who is possibly a member of the media, sucks the energy from people with talent. Kelly shows him in an unflattering light as a parasite that kills what it feeds from: 'Watch your step, he's a gaping hole/Gutless wonder will suck your soul'.

Key point

Kelly shows us that celebrity life can be unexpectedly difficult due to the enormous expectations placed upon a star. In addition, celebrities may be prone to exploitation by unscrupulous characters.

Travelling

Key quotes

'And all around me felt like all inside me/And my body left me and my soul went running' (p.3, 'From St Kilda to Kings Cross')

'Roll on, roll on into the dark night/Leaving all my troubles behind/Carrying my soul far far away' (p.265, 'Wish I Was a Train')

'He was shaking in his seat, riding through the streets/In a Silvertop to her door' (p.57, 'To Her Door')

Kelly has often been praised for the way that he celebrates Australian places in his songs. His characters tend to have strong attachments to place, but they also undertake a significant amount of travel. The travelling song is a common one within popular music and Kelly's oeuvre is no exception. Often the characters experience epiphanies in the moments of transition between one place and another. The in-between space of a car, bus or train can provide a degree of solitude in which characters can make important decisions or come to terms with their circumstances.

Sometimes travel is celebrated for its own sake, providing a change of scene and a scenic backdrop for the expression of feelings. In 'From St Kilda to Kings Cross' (p.3), a man travelling on a bus feels as if he has floated free of his body. Watching the white lines of the road rushing past lulls him into a meditative state, which prompts him to express his fondness for the St Kilda landscape.

Trains

Trains are a common feature of Kelly's songwriting, especially in early albums such as *Post* (1985). The use of a train in a song can be read as a metaphor for mental states. 'Luck' (p.8) is a thinly disguised account of a heroin addict breaking up with his girlfriend because he has to catch a 'train'. Trains can also be metaphors for impending doom, as in 'Dumb Things' (p.49), when the narrator recounts his pig-headed path to destruction: 'Heard the train coming, stayed out on the track'.

The song 'Wish I Was a Train' (p.265) focuses on the narrator's lifelong love of trains, which has brought him comfort in harsh circumstances. Once again, the train is depicted as a vehicle capable of transforming sadness into contentment. In fact, the speaker wishes to become one with a train after death, his spirit 'rid[ing] on the boxcar of an ever-rolling train'. The simpler 'Last Train to Heaven' (p.21) depicts a person's train trip to the afterworld, as the title suggests.

Returning home

In 'To Her Door' (p.57), an estranged husband and father travels back home to his family by bus and taxi, worrying about the outcome of his visit along the way. Leaving his exiled status and returning home to an uncertain future, he is understandably hesitant. Even the action of walking feels strange to him, reflecting his delicate frame of mind: 'He came in on a Sunday, every muscle aching/Walking in slow motion like he'd just been hit'. The fatigue of travel is compounded by his feelings of anxiety and apprehension as he prepares to arrive at his destination.

Car journeys

Car journeys are usually depicted as carefree, as in 'Love Never Runs on Time' (p.144) and 'Under the Sun' (p.58), in which the characters enjoy the freedom of being on the road. Of course, there is always another theme operating underneath the apparently simple travel narrative. The character in 'Love Never Runs on Time' laments the end of a relationship while driving and singing, finding his own way of coming to terms with his loss. In a similarly melancholy tone, 'Under the Sun' tells of the joys of a road trip undertaken by good friends before their friendship came to an end.

Key point

Travel provides space for characters to reflect on the past and make plans for the future. They may also experience significant revelations during the journey.

ESSAY TOPICS

1. 'Vexed relationships between men and women recur throughout Kelly's lyrics.' Discuss.
2. "Even through the darkest night/She can save me from myself … "
   'Female figures in Kelly's lyrics are often figments of a man's imagination rather than fully realised characters.'
   Do you agree?
3. "Going about my father's business/Doing my father's time/What's done to me I'll do to mine … "
   What is the role of inheritance in relation to father figures in Kelly's lyrics?
4. "You might feel something rushing/It's only nothing/Just invisible me … "
   What role do ghostly presences play in Kelly's lyrics?
5. "And all around me felt like all inside me/And my body left me and my soul went running … "
   'Kelly's characters often experience key insights while travelling.' Discuss.
6. 'Kelly's lyrics show the importance of human companionship in the face of death.' Discuss.
7. "In the land of the little kings/There's a price on everything/And everywhere the little kings/Are getting away with murder … "
   'Kelly's lyrics suggest that the power and greed of governments often lead to ordinary people lacking the means to change things.' Discuss.
8. "Once I had a place I could call my own/Now wherever I lay my head is home … "
   'Kelly shows that the stories of the lost and dispossessed are meaningful for all of society.' Discuss.
9. "Well I look so fine/But I feel so low … "
   How do Kelly's lyrics explore the difference between people's outward appearances and their internal emotional states?

10 'Kelly suggests that people cope with their own powerlessness by seeking solace in love.' Discuss.

Analysing a sample topic

'Kelly's lyrics show the importance of human companionship in the face of death.' Discuss.

Analysing the topic

- The phrase 'the importance of human companionship' suggests that friendly company is an essential element of life.
- The phrase 'in the face of death' implies that Kelly's characters are coming to terms with their own mortality, or the deaths of others.
- Select lyrics that feature the themes of both companionship and death. Here, 'I Wasted Time' and 'The Pretty Place' are used as examples.
- Consider these characters' attitudes towards their own deaths. Are they fearful or calm about what will happen to them?

Introduction

Use the following points in writing the introduction.

- Clearly address the topic.
- Express your principal ideas as a strong statement or 'main contention'.
- Include the key points to be covered in the body paragraphs.

Sample introduction (see over)

- The topic statement is referred to in the first and last sentences, clearly showing that the essay is responding to the topic.
- The main contention (italicised) is the last sentence in this example, although it may be placed anywhere in the introduction. Making it the last sentence means you can easily link the introduction with the topic sentence of the first body paragraph.

> In Paul Kelly's lyrics, some characters are shown to require companionship as death approaches. His protagonists often feel lonely and isolated while contemplating their own demise. These protagonists may regret their wasted lives, while others reflect on happier times. Friendship – either in the form of a friend's presence or in the form of memory – is shown to be one of the only distractions from the painful uncertainty the characters experience. *Through his exploration of human behaviour, Kelly shows that people need to forge bonds with others, especially when anticipating the end of their lives.*

Body of essay

- The topic sentence in each paragraph indicates the main idea to be developed.
- Remember to link the last sentence of one paragraph with the topic sentence of the next.
- With song lyrics, you can use one song to establish your argument, then compare and contrast it with another song in the next paragraph.

First body paragraph

- Suggested topic sentence:

  > In 'I Wasted Time', the protagonist regrets the way he has lived his life and seeks companionship to make him feel better about his impending death.

- Develop this idea by describing why he feels the need for human company.
- What is the significance of the phrase 'I cheated time and now it's time to pay'?
- The last sentence of the paragraph should sum up your main ideas and set up a link to the following paragraph.

Second main paragraph

- The topic sentence should introduce a second song, in this case 'The Pretty Place'.
- An effective strategy is to use a linking phrase, such as:

> Just as the protagonist in 'I Wasted Time' desires company to distract him from death, the narrator in 'The Pretty Place' invites a friend to remember happier times in a favourite place.

- The narrator remembers this place because it reminds him of the pleasures of youthful companionship.

Third main paragraph

- Compare and contrast the two songs.
- The songs are similar in that both protagonists draw on their memories to show their longing for companionship as they are facing death.
- The songs are contrasting in that the protagonist in 'I Wasted Time' regrets the way he lived his life, whereas the character in 'A Pretty Place' feels more positively about the quality of his contact with others.

Conclusion

- Summarise your main points, relating them to the topic.
- Restate your main contention.
- The last sentence could be a statement about what Kelly is trying to convey about human experience through these characters.

REFERENCES & READING

The text

Kelly, P 2004, *Don't Start Me Talking: Lyrics 1984–2004*, revised edition, Allen & Unwin, Sydney. First edition published 1999.

References

Aiton, D 1998, 'Dancing in shadows', *The Age*, 10 May, https://web.archive.org/web/20041028061650/https://www.paulkelly.com.au/articles/theage-980510.html

Carney, S 1994, 'Kelly Country', *Rolling Stone* (Aus), no. 498, https://web.archive.org/web/20040208221318/https://www.paulkelly.com.au/articles/rs-9407.html

'From St Kilda to Kings Cross' 1999, *TNT*, 10 August, https://web.archive.org/web/20041225181917/www.paulkelly.com.au/articles/tnt-990810.html

Kelly, P 1993, *Lyrics*, Angus & Robertson, Sydney.

Sammut, C 1999, 'The gentle dreams of an urban troubadour', *Herald Sun*, 15 August, https://web.archive.org/web/20050421221320/http://www.paulkelly.com.au/articles/herald-sun-990815.html

Stevenson, A 2001, 'Blue Notes', *The Age*, 5 October, https://web.archive.org/web/20041223071140/www.paulkelly.com.au/articles/smh-011005.html

Webb, C 2002, 'Women mess with "thrilled" Kelly', *The Age*, 13 May, https://www.theage.com.au/entertainment/music/women-mess-with-thrilled-kelly-20020513-gdu7az.html

Further reading/viewing

http://www.paulkelly.com.au; this is the official website of Paul Kelly.

One Night the Moon 2001, motion picture, Australian Broadcasting Corporation. Directed by Rachel Perkins.